CAPE POETRY PAPERBACKS

ROGER McGOUGH
WAVING AT TRAINS

Roger McGough

WAVING AT TRAINS

JONATHAN CAPE
THIRTY BEDFORD SQUARE LONDON

First published 1982
Copyright © 1982 by Roger McGough

Jonathan Cape Ltd, 30 Bedford Square, London
WC1

British Library Cataloguing in Publication Data

McGough, Roger
Waving at trains. — (Cape poetry paperback)
I. Title
821.'8   PR6063.A219

ISBN 0–224–02058–7

Note

'Six Shooters' first appeared in *Ambit,* and 'The Pope Blesses the Cosmic Force' in *New Departures.* The series of thirteen poems entitled 'Unlucky for Some' was first published by Turret Books. Quotation of the newspaper report in 'Rabbit in Mixer Survives' is by permission of the *Daily Telegraph.*

Printed in Great Britain by
Mackays of Chatham Ltd

For H.B.C.

Contents

You and I   9
Educating Rita   10
Waving at Trains   12
Rainbow   13
When I Am Dead   14
Six Shooters   15
I Don't Like the Poems   21
Water, Tree, Cave, Mother   22
The Scarecrow   23
Noah's Arc   24
There Was a Knock on the Door.
   It Was the Meat.   26
The Examination   27
The Birderman   28
Romantic   30
Is My Team Playing   31
Framed   33
What My Lady Did   34
Shy   35
A Visit to the Poet and his Wife   36
The Battle of Bedford Square   37
Limerick   39
Two Haiku   40
Scintillate   41
The Pope Blesses the Cosmic Force   42
Unlucky for Some   43
Rabbit in Mixer Survives   58
Happy Ending   62

You and I

I explain quietly. You
hear me shouting. You
try a new tack. I
feel old wounds reopen.

You see both sides. I
see your blinkers. I
am placatory. You
sense a new selfishness.

I am a dove. You
recognize the hawk. You
offer an olive branch. I
feel the thorns.

You bleed. I
see crocodile tears. I
withdraw. You
reel from the impact.

Educating Rita
(for W.R.)

Come in and welcome. You're the first.
Let me take your things. Go straight through.
Now something to quench the nation's thirst?
There's lager by the crate. A nice Moselle
Local and highly recommended?
Or there's whisky, vodka, gin as well.
When everyone's arrived we'll serve champagne
And wet the baby's head.

God it's hot. Never thought I'd miss rain.
But there you go. The auld country?
Not as much as I thought I would.
Fresh strawberries. Spring perhaps. And Guinness
Which doesn't travel well and never should.
Susan misses it more I believe.
The way ex-Scousers talk about the place
You wonder why they leave:
'Ferries across the Mersey, the old Pier 'Ead,
Chip butties, the Kop, six in a bed,
The "gents" in the Phil, a cathedral to spare,
Liver birds with long fair hair.'
And going on and on about the native wit
You'd think the buggers had invented it.
But deep down she's no regrets I'm sure.
She needed new friends, a fresh challenge.
She's her own woman now, more mature.
She'll be down in a minute with the star of the show.

Oh by the way, the Russells are coming
Whom I think you all know.
Nice couple. Although Willy will insist
On playing guitar and singing when he's pissed.
And exciting news, I think you'll all agree,
There's a real live actress coming too
Who's starred in a West End theatre show.
Filming out here, just passing through.
So all you sheilas take real good care
Lest Bruce or Norm disappear from the parlour
Into the yard to show her a Koala bear.

No thanks, I've given up. Feel better for it.
Part of Susan's two–year plan for a new and fitter man.
She's even got me jogging. I adore it.
Yes she loves teaching. Can't wait to get back.
And to be honest, neither can I.
Need the money since I got the sack.
Mind you, things couldn't have worked out neater
Means I can spend all my time with the baby
Bringing up and educating Rita. Why Rita?
Just our little secret. A name that binds us.
And here they come now. The two I love the most.
Aren't I a lucky man? Ladies and Gentlemen – A toast!

Waving at Trains

Do people who wave at trains
Wave at the driver, or at the train itself?
Or, do people who wave at trains
Wave at the passengers? Those hurtling strangers,
The unidentifiable flying faces?

They must think we like being waved at.
Children do perhaps, and alone
In a compartment, the occasional passenger
Who is himself a secret waver at trains.
But most of us are unimpressed.

Some even think they're daft.
Stuck out there in a field, grinning.
But our ignoring them, our blank faces,
Even our pulled tongues and up you signs
Come three miles further down the line.

Out of harm's way by then
They continue their walk.
Refreshed and made pure, by the mistaken belief
That their love has been returned,
Because they have not seen it rejected.

It's like God in a way. Another day
Another universe. Always off somewhere.
And left behind, the faithful few,
Stuck out there. Alone in compartments.
All innocence. Arms in the air. Waving.

Rainbow

With a rainbow under your arm
you came a-calling.

A home-made cardboard cut-out.
A spangled boomerang. A gift.

That night we put it on the bed.
Made love, a wish, and slept.

(Later, your rainbows would appear
in bedrooms allover town)

With a rainbow under your arm
you came a-calling.

 A two-dimensional cartoon of the real thing.
Tongue-in-sky. Our love.

When I Am Dead

I could never begin a poem: 'When I am dead'
As several poets still alive have done.
The jokey Last Will, and litanies
Of things we are to do when they have gone.

Courageous stuff. Written I shouldn't wonder
The Morning After, in the throes
Of grim despair. Head still ringing from the noise
Of nights keeling over like glass dominoes.

The chill fear that perhaps the writer
Might outlive the verse, provides the spur
To nail the spectre down in print,
To risk a sort of atheistic prayer.

God, of course, does not appear in rhyme,
Poets of our time being more inclined
To dwell upon the price of manuscripts
And how they want the coffin lined.

Or ashes scattered, cats fed, ex-wives
Gunned down. Meanwhile, in a drawer
Neat and tidy, the bona fide Will,
Drawn-up and witnessed by an old family lawyer.

And though poets I admire have published poems
Whose imperfections reflect our own decay,
I could never begin a poem: 'When I am dead'
In case it tempted Fate, and Fate gave way.

Six Shooters

1   You are his repartee.
     His last word on the subject.

     After each row
     he storms upstairs
     and takes you out of
     the dressingtable drawer.

     He points you
     at the bedroom door
     and waits for her
     to dare one final taunt.

     'Come on up,' you croon.
     'Come on up.'

2   She brazens it out.
     Denies. Tries
     to cover up
     in a negligee of lies.

     You, the lead hyphen
     in between.
     Infiltrator.

     He loves her still
     but she gone done him wrong.
     You burst into song.

     In a flash, all is forgiven.

3   Went through a war together
    never left his side.

    Back home, though illicit,
    still his pride.

    4 a.m. in the den now.
    The note written. Suicide.

    You don't care who
    you kill do you?
    With whom you fellate

    Into whose mouth
    you hurl abuse,
    whose brains you gurgitate.

4   After the outlaw
has bitten the dust
(Never again to rise)

The sheriff
takes you for a spin
round his finger

then blows the smoke
from your eyes.

5   You rarely get the blame.
    Always the man
    behind the hand
    that holds you

    Always the finger
    in front of the trigger
    you squeeze.

    You rarely get the blame.
    Always the fool
    who thinks that you're
    the answer

    Always the tool
    who does just as
    you please.

6   oiled
     and snug
     in a
     moist
     holster

     six
     deadly pearls
     in a
     gross
     oyster

I Don't Like the Poems

I don't like the poems they're making me write
I really don't like them at all
Hierograffiti I don't understand
Scrawled on a hologrammed wall.

They wake me up in the middle of the night
I really don't like them one bit
Dictating mysterious messages
That I am forced to transmit.

Messages with strange metaphors, ass-
onance, similes and the like.
Internal rhymes that chime, and alas
External ones that sometimes don't quite make it.

I don't like the poems they filter through me
Using words I never would use
Like 'filter', 'hierograffiti', 'alien'
I'm enslaved by an alien muse.

*   *   *

And I notice, just lately, at readings
That friends whose work I have known
Unknowingly have started to write
In a similarly haunted tone.
Stumbling over poems we have to recite
In handwriting that isn't our own.

Water, Tree, Cave, Mother

This is the water
cold and black
that drowned the child
that climbed on its back

This is the tree
badtempered and tall
that tripped the child
and made it fall

This is the cave
with rotting breath
that hid the child
and starved it to death

This is the mother
who one day chose
to smother the child
with kisses, and blows and blows and blows.

The Scarecrow

The scarecrow is a scarey crow
Who guards a private patch
Waiting for a trespassing
Little girl to snatch

Spitting soil into her mouth
His twiggy fingers scratch
Pulls her down on to the ground
As circling birdies watch

Drags her to his hidey-hole
And opens up the hatch
Throws her to the crawlies
Then double locks the latch

The scarecrow is a scarey crow
Always out to catch
Juicy bits of compost
To feed his cabbage patch

So don't go where the scarecrows are
Don't go there, Don't go there
Don't go where the scarecrows are
Don't go, Don't go . . .

Don't go where the scarecrows are
Don't go there, Don't go there
Don't go where the scarecrows are
Don't go . . .

Noah's Arc

In my fallout shelter I have enough food
For at least three months. Some books,
Scrabble, and games for the children.
Calor gas and candles. Comfortable beds
And a chemical toilet. Under lock and key
The tools necessary for a life after death.
I have carried out my instructions to the letter.

Most evenings I'm down here. Checking the stores,
Our suits, breathing apparatus. Cleaning
And polishing. My wife, bless her,
Thinks I'm obsessive – like other men
About cars or football. But deep down
She understands. I have no hobbies.
My sole interest is survival.

Every few weeks we have what I call D.D.,
Or Disaster Drill. At the sound of the alarm
We each go about our separate duties:
Disconnecting services, switching off the mains,
Filling the casks with fresh water, etc.
Mine is to oversee everything before finally
Shooting the dog. (This I mime in private.)

At first, the young ones enjoyed the days
And nights spent below. It was an adventure.
But now they're at a difficult age
And regard extinction as the boring concern
Of grown-ups. Like divorce and accountancy.
But I am firm. Daddy knows best
And one fine day they'll grow to thank me.

Beneath my bunk I keep an Armalite rifle
Loaded and ready to use one fine day
When panicking neighbours and so-called friends
Try to clamber aboard. The ones who scoff,
Who ignore the signs. I have my orders,
There will be no stowaways. No gatecrashers
At my party. A party starting soon.

And the sooner the better. Like a grounded
Astronaut I grow daily more impatient.
Am on tenterhooks. Each night
I ask the Lord to get on with it.
I fear sometimes He has forsaken us,
We His favourite children. Meek, drilled,
And ready to inherit an earth, newly-cleansed.

I scan the headlines, watch the screen.
A doctor thrilling at each fresh tumour:
The latest invasion, a breakdown of talks.
I pray for malignancy. The self-induced
Sickness for which there is only one cure:
Radium treatment. The final absolution.
That part of full circle we have yet to come.

There Was a Knock on the Door.
It Was the Meat.

There was a knock on the door.
It was the meat. I let it in.
Something freshly slaughtered
Dragged itself into the hall.

Into the living-room it crawled.
I followed. Though headless,
It headed for the kitchen
As if following a scent.

Straight to the oven it went
And lay there. Oozing softly to itself.
Though moved, I moved inside
And opened wide the door.

I switched to Gas Mark Four.
Set the timer. And grasping
The visitor by a stump
Humped it home and dry.

Did I detect a gentle sigh?
A thank you? The thought that I
Had helped a thing in need
Cheered me as I turned up the heat.

Two hours later the bell rang.
It was the meat.

The Examination

'Well doctor, what do you think?'
He took the poem and examined it.
'Mmmm . . . '
The clock ticked nervously.
'This will have to come out for a start.'
He stabbed a cold finger into its heart.
'Needs cutting here as well.
This can go.
And this is weak. Needs building up.'
He paused . . .
'But it's the Caesura I'm afraid,
Can't do much about that.'
My palms sweated.
'Throw it away and start again, that's my advice.
And on the way out, send in the next patient, will you?'

I buttoned up my manuscript and left.
Outside, it was raining odes and stanzas.
I caught a crowded anthology and went directly home.

Realizing finally that I would never be published.
That I was to remain one of the alltime great unknown poets,
My work rejected by even the vanity presses,
I decided to end it all.

Taking an overdose of Lyricism
I awaited the final peace
When into the room burst the Verse Squad
Followed by the Poetry Police.

The Birderman

Most weekends, starting in the spring
Until late summer, I spend angling.
Not for fish. I find that far too tame
But for birds, a much more interesting game.

A juicy worm I use as bait
Cast a line into the tree and wait.
Seldom for long (that's half the fun)
A commotion in the leaves, the job's half done.

Pull hard, jerk home the hook
Then reel him in. Let's have a look . . .
A tiny thing, a fledgling, young enough to spare.
I show mercy. Unhook, and toss it to the air.

It flies nestwards and disappears among the leaves
(What man roasts and braises, he too reprieves).
What next? A magpie. Note the splendid tail.
I wring its neck. Though stringy, it'll pass for quail.

Unlike water, the depths of trees are high
So, standing back, I cast into the sky.
And ledger there beyond the topmost bough,
Until threshing down, like a black cape, screams a crow!

Evil creature! A witch in feathered form.
I try to net the dark, encircling storm.
It caws for help. Its cronies gather round
They curse and swoop. I hold my ground.

An infernal mass, a black, horrific army
I'll not succumb to Satan's origami.
I reach into my coat, I've come prepared,
Bring out my pocket scarecrow – Watch out bird!

It's cross-shaped, the sign the godless fear
In a thunderflap of wings they disappear.
Except of course, that one, ungainly kite
Broken now, and quickly losing height.

I haul it in, and with a single blow
Dispatch it to that Aviary below.
The ebb and flow: magpie, thrush, nightingale and crow.
The wood darkens. Time to go.

I pack away the food I've caught
And thankful for a good day's sport
Amble home. The forest fisherman.
And I'll return as soon as I can

To bird. For I'm a birderer. The birderman.

Romantic

I'm a romantic.
I often want to bring you flowers
Leave notes under the pillow.
Billets doux. Fivers.

I'm a romantic.
Many's the time I've nearly bought
the unexpected gift.
Chocolates. Diamonds.

I'm a romantic.
How often do I think
of surprising you at the sink.
Pulling the wool over your eyes.

I'm a romantic.
Love on the lino: soapy chocolates,
Diamonds, crushed flowers, fivers,
Billets doux. Wool.

(Little packet, two-thirds full.)

Is My Team Playing
(after A.E. Housman)

Is my team playing
That I used to cheer
Each Saturday on the terrace
Before I transferred here?

Aye the lads still battle
They go from strength to strength
Won the FA cup
Since you were laid at length.

Is factory still closed
With pickets at the gate?
Would I could lend a hand
Ere I felt the hand of Fate.

No things are back to normal
Thanks to the TUC
Our wages now are frozen
But not so much as thee.

And my lonely widow
Does she nightly grieve
For her dear departed
Gone early to the grave?

No she's right as rain
And not the one to weep
She is well looked after
Be still my lad, and sleep.

And what of you, dear friend
Are you still unwed
Or have you found a lady
To share your bachelor bed?

Well . . . er I don't know how to say this
But after the funeral your wife was upset
So we had a few jars
Went back to yours and

Wor, you lousy get!

Framed

In the Art Gallery
it is after closing time
everybody has left
except a girl
who is undressing
in front of a large painting
entitled: 'Nude'

(The girl undressing
is the girl in the painting)

naked now she faces
the girl who gazes
out at the girl
who naked faces
the girl who
naked gazes out

of the picture
steps the nude
who smiles, dresses and walks away
leaving the naked girl
gazing into the empty space
Framed   by this poem.

What My Lady Did

I asked my lady what she did
  She gave me a silver flute and smiled.
A musician I guessed, yes that would explain
  Her temperament so wild.

I asked my lady what she did
  She gave me a comb inlaid with pearl.
A hairdresser I guessed, yes that would explain
  Each soft and billowing curl.

I asked my lady what she did
  She gave me a skein of wool and left.
A weaver I guessed, yes that would explain
  Her fingers long and deft.

I asked my lady what she did
  She gave me a slipper trimmed with lace.
A dancer I guessed, yes that would explain
  Her suppleness and grace.

I asked my lady what she did
  She gave me a picture not yet dry.
A painter I guessed, yes that would explain
  The steadiness of her eye.

I asked my lady what she did
  She gave me a fountain pen of gold.
A poet I guessed, yes that would explain
  The strange stories that she told.

I asked my lady what she did
  She told me – and oh, the grief!
I should have guessed, she's under arrest
  My lady was a thief!

Shy

The shy girl at the party
turned out to be

the shy girl in the car
turned out to be

the shy girl in the bedroom
turned out to be

with the light
turned out to be

shyning!

A Visit to the Poet and his Wife

To set the scene: A cave
in Madron, Cornwall.
On a warm September afternoon
Mr and Mrs W.S.G. are 'at home'
to admirers bearing distilled gifts.

Mine host, after clearing
a mess of mss from the table
takes *implements in their places*
from its place, and puts on
spectacles to clear the air.

A warm, brown voice
with silver whiskers unveils
a poem that is the spitting
image of itself. The onlisteners
are amazed at its likeness.

Tumblers, half-filled with malt,
are topped up with bright
watery sunshine by the good
Lady of the Cottage. The afternoon
saddens at its own passing.

To set the scene: A cave
in Madron, Cornwall.
On a warm September afternoon
Mr and Mrs W.S.G. are 'at home'
to admirers bearing distilled gifts.

The Battle of Bedford Square

At a publishing party in Bedford Square
The critic is at ease
With lots of lady novelists
To flatter and to tease

He's witty, irresistible,
Completely on the ball
A few more wines, who knows,
He might make love to them all

But one by one they disappear
With a smile, and a promise to phone
And suddenly it's midnight
And suddenly he's alone

He surveys the litter, arty,
In search of a back to stab
Anger jangling inside him
Like an undigested kebab

Across the ashen carpet
He staggers, glass in hand
And corners a northern poet
Whose verses he can't stand

As if a bell had sounded
A space had quickly cleared
They were in a clinch and fighting
And the waiters, how they cheered

There was a flurry of books and mss
Bruises on the waxen fruit
A right to a left-over agent
Blood on the publisher's suit

A hook to a Booker Prize runner-up
A left to a right-wing hack
A straight to the heart of the matter
And the critic's on his back

An uppercut to an uppercrust diarist
From an anthropologist, pissed,
An Art Editor's head in collision
With a Marketing Manager's fist

Two novelists gay, were soon in the fray
Exchanging blow for blow
As the battle seeped into the Square
Like a bloodstain into snow

And though, at last, the police arrived
They didn't intervene
'What a way to launch a book.
Bloody typical Bloomsbury scene!'

All that now of course is history
And people come from far and wide
To see the spot where literary
Giants fought and died

Holding cross-shaped paper bookmarks
They mouth a silent prayer
In memory of those who fell
At the Battle of Bedford Square.

Limerick

There was a young lady from Dingle,
Who liked music that made her all tingle,
And she really did rave,
About the song of the cave,
(you know, the Mendelssohn one about Fingal).

Two Haiku

only trouble with
Japanese haiku is that
You write one, and then

only seventeen
syllables later you want
to write another.

Scintillate

I have outlived
my youthfulness
So a quiet life for me.

Where once
I used to
scintillate

now I sin
till ten
past three.

The Pope Blesses the Cosmic Force

s . . . . . . pace

in . . . . . vade . . . . rs

in   vade

                      pace . . . . m

Unlucky For Some

1   What do I do for a living? Survive.

Simple as that. 'God helps those

who help themselves.' That's what the

vicar told me. So I went into

the supermarket and helped myself.

Got six months. God help those

who help themselves. Nowadays

I'm a traveller. South-west mainly

then back here for the winter.

I like the open air. Plenty of it

and it's free. Everything else I beg

borrow or steal. Keep just about alive.

What do I do for a living? Survive.

2   It runs like duck's water off me back.

What people say. How do they know?

They seem to think I enjoy

looking shabby. Having no money.

Being moved on from cafés,

from warm places. How would

they like it? They'd soon sneer

on the other side of their faces

if they ended up down and out.

Up down and out. Up and down.

Out of luck. That's all you have to be.

Half of them calling the kettle black.

It runs like duck's water off me back.

3   It's the addicts I can't stand.

Getting drunk on pills. Stoned

they call it. Make me sick.

Sticking needles into themselves

in dirty lavatories. Got no shame.

And they get prescriptions. Wish

my doctor would give me one

everytime I felt like a drink.

I could take it along to the

allnight off-licence in Piccadilly

come back here and get drunk

for a week. Get high. Stoned.

It's the addicts I can't stand.

4   I'm no good, that's what I've been told

ever since I can remember. So

I try to live up to my reputation.

Or down to it. Thievin' mainly.

And drugs. You get used to prison.

Don't like it though, being cooped up.

That's why I couldn't work in a shop

or a factory. Drive me crazy.

Can't settle down. 21 years old

and I look 40. It's the drugs.

I'll O.D. probably. Couldn't care less.

Rather die young than grow old.

I'm no good, that's what I've been told.

5   Now I'm one of the idle poor.

A rose in a garden of weeds.

Slightly shrivelled of course, but nevertheless

an interesting species: *'Retrobata Inebriata'*.

I was born into the leisured classes.

No doubt you can tell. Born rich

and married rich as well. Too much

leisure that was the trouble. And drink.

Cost me a husband, home, family.

Now I've only a bed, a roof over my head.

Perhaps I don't deserve more.

I used to be one of the idle rich.

Now I'm one of the idle poor.

6   I get frightened you see. Easily scared.

Trouble is, I know what's goin' on.

The things they've got planned.

The others don't understand, you see.

They say: 'What are you scared of?

There's no need to be frightened.'

I huddle myself up against

the window sometimes. Like a curtain.

Listening to what's goin' on outside.

I've got X-ray hearin', you see.

It stretches for miles. When people

talk about me, I can hear every word.

I get frightened you see. Easily scared.

7   First and foremost I need a coat.

The one I'm wearing's got patches

on the patches. I can't go

for interviews dressed like this.

What sort of a job do you think

I'd get? A job as a tramp?

No thank you. And while I'm here

I need some vests and knickers.

None of them fancy ones either.

And shoes. Two pair. Leather.

Don't argue, I know my rights.

Refuse and I'll take you to court.

First and foremost I need a coat.

8   I try to take up little space.

Keep myself to myself. I find

the best way to get by is to say

nothing. Don't argue, don't interfere.

When there's trouble lie low.

That's why I wear a lot of grey.

Helps me hide away. Blend in

against the background. I eat

very little. Don't smoke or drink.

Get through the day unnoticed

that's the trick. The way to heaven.

Say me prayers each night just in case.

I try to take up little space.

9   It may sound silly but it's true.

I drink like there was no tomorrow

and I can't stand the taste of the stuff.

Never have. My mother was a drunk

and the smell of her was enough.

I drink to forget. I know it's a cliché

but it's true. I drink to forget

and I do. Occasionally I remember

what I was trying not to remember

but by then I've remembered

to drink, in order to make

myself forget. And I do.

It may sound silly but it's true.

10   I would have liked children I suppose.

A family and that. It's natural.

But it's too late now. Too old.

And trouble is I never liked men.

If I'd been born pretty

or with a nice figure, I might

have liked them then. Men,

and sex and that. But I'm

no oil painting. Had to face

that fact right from the start.

And you see, if you're born ugly

well that's the way life goes. But

I would have liked children I suppose.

11   Oh no, I don't have to be here.

I'm not a cast-off like the rest.

I'm one of the lucky ones. I've got

children. Both grown up. A son

and daughter who'd be only too pleased

to have me living with them.

But I prefer my independence.

Besides, they've got their own lives.

I'd only have to pick up the phone

and they'd be over. Or send money.

I mean, I could afford a room

in a nice clean hotel somewhere.

Oh no, I don't have to be here.

12   Things are better now with me new glasses.

I got the last pair just after the war

and I think they'd lost their power.

If I could read I'd be able

to read even better now. Everything's

so much clearer. Faces and places.

Television's improved too. Not

that I'm one for stayin' in.

I prefer to be out and about.

Sightseein' and windowshoppin'.

In and out of the traffic.

If you keep on the move, time soon passes.

Things are better now, with me new glasses.

13   I always wanted to go on the stage.

Dancer mainly, though I had a lovely voice.

Ran away to the bright lights of London

to be a star. Nothing came of it though,

so I went on the game. An actress

of sorts you might say. I'm the oldest

professional in the oldest profession.

Would you like to see me dance?

I'll dance for you. I dance in here

all the time. The girls love it.

Do you like my dancing? Round

and round. Not bad eh? For my age.

I always wanted to go on the stage.

Rabbit in Mixer Survives

A baby rabbit fell into a quarry's mixing machine yesterday and came out in the middle of a concrete block. But the rabbit still had the strength to dig its way free before the block set.

The tiny creature was scooped up with 30 tons of sand, then swirled and pounded through the complete mixing process. Mr Michael Hooper, the machine operator, found the rabbit shivering on top of the solid concrete block, its coat stiff with fragments. A hole from the middle of the block and paw marks showed the escape route.

Mr Reginald Denslow, manager of J.R. Pratt and Sons' quarry at Kilmington, near Axminster, Devon, said: 'This rabbit must have a lot more than nine lives to go through this machine. I just don't know how it avoided being suffocated, ground, squashed or cut in half.' With the 30 tons of sand, it was dropped into a weighing hopper and carried by conveyor to an overhead mixer where it was whirled around with gallons of water.

From there the rabbit was swept to a machine which hammers wet concrete into blocks by pressure of 100 lb per square inch. The rabbit was encased in a block eighteen inches long, nine inches high and six inches thick. Finally the blocks were ejected on to the floor to dry and the dazed rabbit clawed itself free. 'We cleaned him up, dried him by the electric fire, then he hopped away,' Mr Denslow said.

Daily Telegraph

'Tell us a story Grandad'
The bunny rabbits implored
'About the block of concrete
Out of which you clawed.'

'Tell every gory detail
Of how you struggled free
From the teeth of the Iron Monster
And swam through a quicksand sea.'

'How you battled with the Humans
(And the part we like the most)
Your escape from the raging fire
When they held you there to roast.'

The old adventurer smiled
And waved a wrinkled paw
'All right children, settle down
I'll tell it just once more.'

His thin nose started twitching
Near-blind eyes began to flood
As the part that doesn't age
Drifted back to bunnyhood.

When spring was king of the seasons
And days were built to last
When thunder was merely thunder
Not a distant quarry blast.

How, leaving the warren one morning
Looking for somewhere to play,
He'd wandered far into the woods
And there had lost his way.

When suddenly without warning
The earth gave way, and he fell
Off the very edge of the world
Into the darkness of Hell.

Sharp as the colour of a carrot
On a new-born bunny's tongue
Was the picture he recalled
Of that day when he was young.

Trance-formed now by the memory
His voice was close to tears
But the story he was telling
Was falling on deaf ears.

There was giggling and nudging
And lots of 'sssh – he'll hear'
For it was a trick, a game they played
Grown crueller with each year.

'Poor old Grandad' they tittered
As they one by one withdrew
'He's told it all so often
He now believes it's true.'

Young rabbits need fresh carrots
And his had long grown stale
So they left the old campaigner
Imprisoned in his tale.

Petrified by memories
Haunting ever strong
Encased in a block of time
Eighteen inches long.

* * *

Alone in a field in Devon
An old rabbit is sitting, talking,
When out of the wood, at the edge of the world,
A man with a gun comes walking.

Happy Ending

Out of the wood
at the edge of the world
a man with a gun
comes walking.
Feels not the sun
upon his face
nor hears a rabbit talking.

Over the edge
at the end of it all
the man stands
still as stone.
In his hands
the gun held
to his mouth like a microphone.

The rabbit
runs to safety
at the sudden cry
of pain.
As the man lets fly
a ferret
into the warren of his brain.